Fact Finders™

~ The American Colonies ~

The New Hampshire Colony

by Kathleen W. Deady

Consultant:
Matthew H. Crocker
Associate Professor of History
Keene State College
Keene, New Hampshire

press

Mankato, Minnesota

Fact Finders is published by Capstone Press,
151 Good Counsel Drive, P.O. Box 669, Mankato, Minnesota 56002.
www.capstonepress.com

Library of Congress Cataloging-in-Publication Data
Deady, Kathleen W.
　　The New Hampshire colony / by Kathleen W. Deady.
　　p. cm.—(Fact Finders. American colonies)
　　Includes index.
　　ISBN 0-7368-2677-7 (hardcover)
　　1. New Hampshire—History—Colonial period, ca. 1600–1775—Juvenile literature.
　　I. Title. II. Series: American colonies (Capstone Press)
F37.D43 2006
974.2'02—dc22   2004028658

Summary: An introduction to the history, government, economy, resources, and people of
the New Hampshire Colony. Includes maps and charts.

Editorial Credits
Mandy Marx, editor; Jennifer Bergstrom, set designer, illustrator, and book designer;
　　Bobbi J. Dey, book designer; Jo Miller, photo researcher/photo editor

Photo Credits
Cover image: Shipbuilding in New Netherland, Bridgeman Art Library/Ship Building in New
　　Netherland, c. by G. Moore(fl.1930's)/New York Historical Society, New York, USA
Bruce Coleman Inc./Lee Foster, 11
Corbis/Bettmann, 14; North Carolina Museum of Art, 12–13
Corel/Declaration of Independence painting by John Trumball, 27
Getty Images Inc./MPI, 15
Marilyn "Angel" Wynn, 6
Matthew Thompson, 10
National Archives and Records Administration, 29 (right)
North Wind Picture Archives, 4–5, 7, 17, 20–21, 23, 26, 29 (left)
Tom Pantages, 19

1 2 3 4 5 6 10 09 08 07 06 05

Table of Contents

Chapter 1

New Hampshire's First People

Algonquian Indians have called New Hampshire home for thousands of years. Two main groups of Algonquians lived there before Europeans came. They were the Pennacook and the Abenaki tribes.

Algonquian Daily Life

The Algonquian lived in groups of 50 to 200 people. Dome-shaped wigwams provided shelter. For food, women grew corn, beans, and squash. Men hunted deer, bear, and other animals. They also fished in New Hampshire's lakes and rivers. The Algonquian traveled the waterways in canoes hollowed out of tree trunks.

Building wigwams took teamwork.
Men built the frames, and women
made mats to cover the frames.

5

▲ The Algonquian used wooden snowshoes to make winter travel easier.

The land that became New Hampshire has cold, snowy winters. During winter, the Algonquian wore warm robes made of animal skins. They walked over snow in wooden snowshoes. The snowshoes kept them from sinking into thick snow.

European Arrival

The Algonquian did not believe in owning land. They used land for farming. When the soil was used up, they moved to find better land.

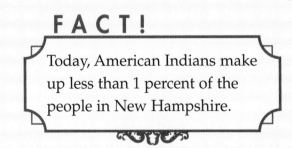

FACT!

Today, American Indians make up less than 1 percent of the people in New Hampshire.

Europeans came to the area in the early 1600s. The Algonquian did not understand when the settlers tried to buy their land. They thought they were receiving gifts. The Algonquian shared the land. They even taught survival skills to the new settlers. Without the Algonquian, New Hampshire's first colonists may have died.

The Algonquian were a great help to New Hampshire's first settlers. ⬇

Chapter 2

Early Settlers

By the 1600s, France and Spain had formed colonies in the Americas. The Spanish found gold in their colonies. Animals in the French colonies supplied valuable furs. At that time, James I was England's king. He wanted his country to benefit from this new land as well.

In 1619, King James I formed the Council for New England. This group gave people land in North America. In 1622, the council gave land to John Mason and Sir Ferdinando Gorges. In 1629, Mason and Gorges divided their land. Mason chose the southern part. He called it New Hampshire. Gorges' land later became the state of Maine.

Colonial borders were set in 1763. New Hampshire and New York disagreed on their borders. ➡

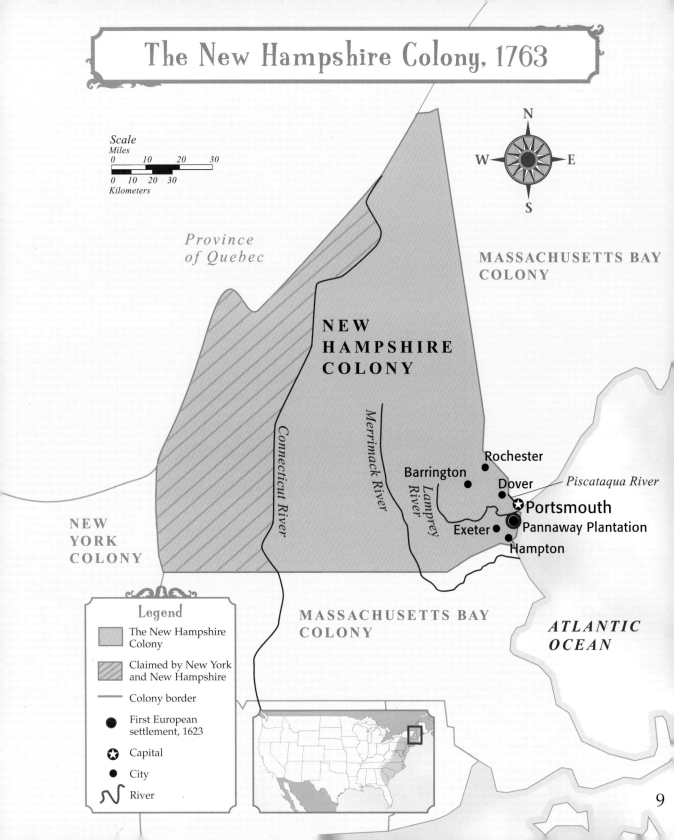

The New Hampshire Colony, 1763

Scale
Miles
0   10   20   30
0   10   20   30
Kilometers

N
W   E
S

Province of Quebec

MASSACHUSETTS BAY
COLONY

**NEW
HAMPSHIRE
COLONY**

Connecticut River

Merrimack River

Lamprey River

Rochester

Barrington

Dover

Piscataqua River

⭐ Portsmouth

Exeter   Pannaway Plantation

Hampton

NEW
YORK
COLONY

MASSACHUSETTS BAY
COLONY

*ATLANTIC
OCEAN*

Legend

▨	The New Hampshire Colony
▨	Claimed by New York and New Hampshire
—	Colony border
●	First European settlement, 1623
✪	Capital
•	City
∿	River

9

↟ Pannaway Plantation was a small fishing village on the coast of New Hampshire.

First Settlements

Mason waited to send settlers to New Hampshire until 1630. Meanwhile, other people settled there.

In 1623, David Thomson received a land **grant**. Later that year he built Pannaway Plantation. It was located on New Hampshire's coast. People there caught fish and sold them to English traders.

Also in 1623, Edward Hilton founded Hilton's Point. He broke the law by starting a town without a land grant. The Council for New England forgave him in 1631. Hilton's Point was given legal standing.

Finally, in 1630, Mason sent people to the area. They settled at a spot along the Piscataqua River. This area was filled with wild strawberries. The settlers named the town Strawberry Banke. Today, it is known as Portsmouth.

Government

As settlements grew, the towns needed a central government. In 1641, the Massachusetts Bay Colony took over New Hampshire. In 1679, King Charles II divided the two areas. He made New Hampshire an official royal colony.

FACT!

Hilton's Point, now called Dover, is New Hampshire's longest lasting settlement.

Many colonial buildings still stand in Portsmouth as part of the Strawberry Banke Museum. ⬇

Chapter 3

Colonial Life

Farming was a necessary part of life for early settlers. New Hampshire's land was rocky and covered with forests. Settlers had to cut trees before they could plant crops. They also had to dig large stones out of the soil.

Colonial Daily Life

The first New Hampshire colonists worked hard. Men farmed, fished, and hunted. Women worked in gardens and cooked meals, while caring for children. They made soap and candles. They also sewed clothes for their families.

New Hampshire colonists built homes and farms out of a rocky wilderness.

Some children in the New Hampshire Colony went to school. Many schools were built when Massachusetts ruled the colony. Massachusetts law said towns with 50 or more families must hire teachers.

Fighting for Land

As more people came, the Algonquian lost more land. Settlers used confusing treaties or just moved on to Algonquian land. Feeling cheated, the Algonquian attacked settlers. The settlers returned the attacks. This fighting went on for years.

◀ Schools in the New Hampshire Colony taught basic reading, writing, and math.

France also had colonies in North America. Between 1689 and 1763, Britain fought France for its North American land. Many American Indians sided with the French. These bloody battles are called the French and Indian wars. New Hampshire served as a main battleground. In 1763, Britain won. They pushed the Algonquian west and took over France's land in North America.

Many New Hampshire towns were attacked in the French and Indian wars. ⬇

Chapter 4

Work and Trade

Farming was not the only work in New Hampshire. Many settlers were fishers or fur traders. Coastal waters were filled with cod and other fish. New Hampshire's forests supplied trappers with beaver furs. The colonists traded fish and furs to Europeans. In return, they were given much needed supplies.

By the late 1600s, New Hampshire's lumber industry was booming. Pine, maple, cedar, and birch trees grew in New Hampshire forests. Colonists used these trees to build homes and boats. Many New England towns had buildings made with lumber from New Hampshire.

New Hampshire colonists worked hard to provide lumber for buildings and ships.

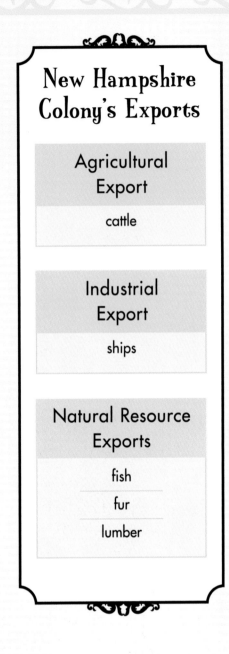

New Hampshire Colony's Exports

Agricultural Export

cattle

Industrial Export

ships

Natural Resource Exports

fish

fur

lumber

The most prized trees in the colony were white pines. These trees grow more than 100 feet (30 meters) tall. They were perfect as **masts** on sailing ships. Many white pines were used for English navy ships.

A Growing Economy

Shipbuilding businesses opened all along the coast. Coastal towns grew, and more businesses opened up. Portsmouth was one of the cities that grew. In 1679, it became the colony's capital.

By the early 1700s, lumbering and shipbuilding were New Hampshire's biggest businesses. About 90 sawmills made lumber for ships. The Lamprey and the Piscataqua Rivers powered many of these sawmills.

New Hampshire's sawmills pumped out lumber for many buildings in New England. ▼

Chapter 5

Community and Faith

Most New Hampshire towns were built around the meetinghouse. Settlers talked about important matters and voted on town laws there. On Sundays, they used the meetinghouse for church. During services, colonists sang hymns, and preachers gave powerful sermons.

New Hampshire's first settlers came to fish and trade. But soon, religious freedom brought people there.

In the Massachusetts Bay Colony, **Puritans** ran the government. Anyone who disagreed with the Puritan way of life was punished.

The meetinghouse was the central gathering place in most New Hampshire towns.

An Unlikely Refuge

Many Massachusetts colonists came to New Hampshire to escape strict Puritan rules. Even when Massachusetts controlled New Hampshire, religious laws were often ignored. People with different beliefs found freedom in New Hampshire. Some of them were Baptists, Quakers, and Presbyterians.

Population Growth of the New Hampshire Colony

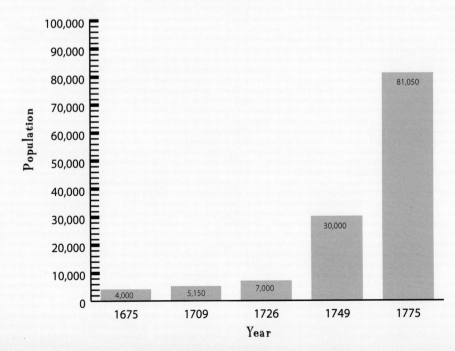

The Massachusetts government even threw out fellow Puritans. Reverend John Wheelwright was sent away for disagreeing with Puritan views. In 1638, he traveled to southeast New Hampshire. Wheelwright bought a village from the Pennacook Indians and started the town of Exeter.

Stephen Bachiler was another outspoken Puritan minister. He was kicked out of Massachusetts in 1639. Later that year, Bachiler founded the town of Hampton near Exeter.

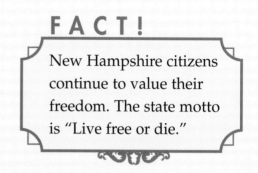

FACT!

New Hampshire citizens continue to value their freedom. The state motto is "Live free or die."

John Wheelwright founded the city of Exeter, New Hampshire. ⬇

~ Chapter 6 ~

Becoming a State

By 1763, American colonists began to dislike Britain's rule. The colonists had defended their land and created their own way of life. New Hampshire colonists had spent years defending their land. They had defeated the Indians and the French. Their victory in the French and Indian wars gave Britain more land. But King George III would not let them settle this land.

Britain also put **taxes** on paper, sugar, and tea. The taxes upset the colonists, since they had no voice in British government. People in other colonies rebelled against the taxes. They threw shiploads of tea into the ocean.

Land claimed by New Hampshire and New York later became the state of Vermont. ➡

The Thirteen Colonies, 1763

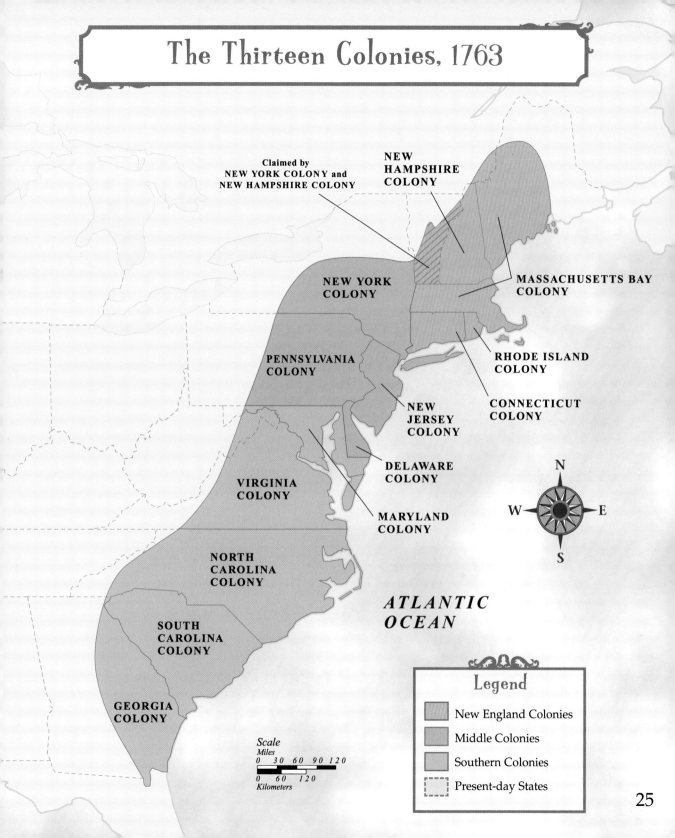

Claimed by
NEW YORK COLONY and
NEW HAMPSHIRE COLONY

NEW
HAMPSHIRE
COLONY

NEW YORK
COLONY

MASSACHUSETTS BAY
COLONY

PENNSYLVANIA
COLONY

RHODE ISLAND
COLONY

NEW
JERSEY
COLONY

CONNECTICUT
COLONY

DELAWARE
COLONY

VIRGINIA
COLONY

MARYLAND
COLONY

NORTH
CAROLINA
COLONY

SOUTH
CAROLINA
COLONY

GEORGIA
COLONY

ATLANTIC
OCEAN

N
W   E
S

Scale
Miles
0   30 60 90 120

0   60   120
Kilometers

Legend
New England Colonies
Middle Colonies
Southern Colonies
Present-day States

New Hampshire is the only one of the 13 American colonies in which no Revolutionary War battle was fought.

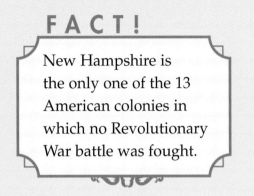

Before the revolution, Governor John Wentworth was a hero in New Hampshire. ▼

At first, New Hampshire colonists were loyal to their royal British governor, John Wentworth. He had helped build roads and schools in the colony. But the colonists discovered Wentworth was giving money to the British army. Feeling betrayed, many New Hampshire colonists joined rebel forces.

In 1774, the colonies sent **representatives** to the Continental Congress. This group tried to reason with Britain. But in 1775, the Revolutionary War (1775-1783) began. Early in July, 1776, Congress approved the Declaration of **Independence**.

Josiah Bartlett, William Whipple, and Matthew Thornton signed the Declaration of Independence for New Hampshire.

Americans fought for their freedom for eight years. General John Stark, from New Hampshire, led soldiers into many battles. In 1783, America won the war. American leaders wrote the **Constitution** of the United States in 1787. It set up the U.S. government. On June 22, 1788, New Hampshire approved the U.S. Constitution. It was the ninth state to join the United States.

Fast Facts

Name

The New Hampshire Colony
(named after Hampshire,
England)

Location

New England colonies

Years of Founding

1622–land grant given to Mason
1623–first settlements

First Settlements

Pannaway Plantation
Hilton's Point

Colony's Founders

John Mason
David Thomson
Edward Hilton

Religious Faiths

Baptist, Presbyterian, Puritan,
Quaker

Agricultural Product

Cattle

Major Industries

Fishing, fur trading, lumber,
shipbuilding

Population in 1775

81,050 people

Statehood

June 22, 1788
(9th state)

Time Line

1630
John Mason sends settlers to start Strawberry Banke, now Portsmouth.

1623
Pannaway Plantation and Hilton's Point are New Hampshire's first settlements.

1622
Council for New England grants charter to John Mason and Sir Ferdinando Gorges.

1641-1679
New Hampshire is governed by Massachusetts Bay colony.

1689
French and Indian wars begin.

1707
An Act of Union unites England, Wales, and Scotland; they become the Kingdom of Great Britain.

1763
British win French and Indian wars; Proclamation of 1763 sets colonial borders and provides land for American Indians.

1775
American colonies begin fight for independence from Great Britain in the Revolutionary War.

1776
Declaration of Independence is approved in July.

1783
America wins the Revolutionary War.

1788
On June 22, New Hampshire is the ninth state to join the United States.

29

Glossary

constitution (kon-stuh-TOO-shuhn)—the written system of laws in a state or country that state the rights of the people and the powers of the government

grant (GRANT)—a gift such as land or money given for a particular purpose

independence (in-di-PEN-duhnss)—being free from the control of other people

mast (MAST)—a tall pole on a ship's deck that holds its sails

Puritan (PYOOR-uh-tuhn)—one of a group of Christians who wanted simple church services and a strict moral code

representative (rep-ri-ZEN-tuh-tiv)—someone who is chosen to speak or act for others

taxes (TAKS-es)—money that people and businesses must pay in order to support a government

Internet Sites

FactHound offers a safe, fun way to find Internet sites related to this book. All of the sites on FactHound have been researched by our staff.

Here's how:

1. Visit *www.facthound.com*
2. Type in this special code **0736826777** for age-appropriate sites. Or enter a search word related to this book for a more general search.
3. Click on the **Fetch It** button.

FactHound will fetch the best sites for you!

Read More

Blohm, Craig E. *New Hampshire.* Thirteen Colonies. San Diego: Lucent Books, 2002.

Davis, Kevin A. *The New Hampshire Colony.* Our Thirteen Colonies. Chanhassen, Minn.: Child's World, 2004.

Nobleman, Marc Tyler. *The Thirteen Colonies.* We the People. Minneapolis: Compass Point Books, 2002.

Index